Old Blair Atholl, Killiecrankie and Struan
Bernard Byrom

A happy party of tourists who've stopped for a group photo in the Pass of Killiecrankie in August 1913.

© Bernard Byrom, 2022
First published in the United Kingdom, 2022,
by Stenlake Publishing Ltd.
www.stenlake.co.uk
ISBN 978-1-84033-929-1

The publishers regret that they cannot supply
copies of any pictures featured in this book.

Printed by
Blissetts, Unit E1-E8 Shield Drive,
West Cross Ind Pk, Brentford, TW8 9EX

Acknowledgements

The author wishes to thank the following for their assistance during the research of this book: Patrick Collins, Research & Enquiries Officer, National Motor Museum Trust, Beaulieu; John Wise, Highland Railway Society; and Sallie at the Blair Atholl Visitor Information Centre.

Bruar Water flows down the steep northern slopes of Glen Garry before discharging into the River Garry at Bruar, three and a half miles west of Blair Atholl. The Falls of Bruar are a series of waterfalls on the Water and have been a tourist attraction since the eighteenth century. They were probably formed sometime in the last 10,000 years after the retreat of the glaciers at the end of the last ice age. The layering of the rocks means that the water has cut a meandering path through the softer rock and left the harder rock untouched. There are two large waterfalls, the highest of which falls perpendicularly about 60 feet, and a number of smaller drops; this picture shows the Lower Falls of Bruar. Robert Burns visited the area in 1797 and, disappointed by the barren moorland surrounding such a lovely spot, afterwards wrote his poem *The Humble Petition of Bruar Water to the Noble Duke of Atholl*. It entreated John Murray, 4th Duke of Atholl, to plant some trees and bushes around the falls. Around ten years after the poet's death in 1796, the Duke finally took the hint and began planting trees as a memorial to Burns. His unique method of planting was to take a cannon onto the hillside, load it with gunpowder and wadding packed with the seeds of Scots Pine and European Larch and blast them across the hillside. The duke also laid out the path that is still in use today and constructed two bridges as viewpoints over the falls, one of which is shown here with four Edwardian tourists admiring the view.

Introduction

The village of Blair Atholl in Perthshire lies in Glen Garry, at the confluence of the River Tilt and the River Garry. It is a relatively recent settlement, dating from the first half of the nineteenth century when General Wade's military road of 1728, which passed through old Blair village, was superseded in 1822 by a new section of road on which a bridge was built nearer the mouth of the River Tilt. The two villages of Bridge of Tilt and Blair Atholl grew up on either side of the river and became known collectively as 'Blair Atholl'.

Wade's road had been built to facilitate the rapid movement of English forces between their garrisons in the Highlands following the 1715 Jacobite Rebellion; years before that, the first Jacobite rising had led to the Battle of Killiecrankie which took place just a few miles south of old Blair village on 27 July 1689. The area's most famous historical event, this was fought between an English army of the Protestant King William of Orange and a Jacobite army which was loyal to the deposed Catholic King James II of England (and VII of Scotland). The English forces were led by General Hugh MacKay of Scourie and the Jacobites, made up of Highland clansmen, were led by the charismatic John Graham of Claverhouse, Viscount Dundee. The Highlanders were outnumbered by about two to one but in the face of their wild charge down the Pass of Killiecrankie no fewer than 2,000 of MacKay's men were killed and 500 made prisoner, while the rest fled. A little way downstream is the famous 'Soldier's Leap' where an English soldier is reputed to have saved himself from pursuing Highlanders by leaping eighteen feet across the river. The Highland army was victorious but their leader, Viscount Dundee, was shot and killed during the battle. Now leaderless, the victory was squandered when a large proportion of the Highland army contented itself with looting the English army's baggage train and then drifted away home. The Jacobite cause was finally defeated at Culloden in 1745.

In early Victorian times the majority of local inhabitants spoke Gaelic. The better-off burned coal in their houses, which was expensive, having to be brought more than thirty miles from Perth. Most others burned peat, which also had to be fetched from a distance. In 1755 the population of the parish had been recorded as 3,257, but by the minister's reckoning it had reduced to about 2,333 by 1836. This reduction of 924 persons (28%) over a period of only 81 years was caused by people moving, or sometimes being evicted, from the higher ground as sheep farms grew larger; they generally moved to the south of the country or to America. As this land-based economy developed, sportsmen from the south trained young men as servants or guides or 'sacketmen', a 'sacket' being a sportsman's game bag. In 1868 the *National Gazetteer* claimed that the forest of Atholl covered an area of 100,000 acres and it was by then a famous hunting ground abounding in red deer and other game.

The arrival of the railway linking Perth with Inverness in 1863 really began the process of bringing the two villages into the modern era. It facilitated the rapid movement of goods throughout the district and, perhaps above all else, facilitated the arrival of tourists who came in droves to enjoy this beautiful area - and still do. The scenes in this book range from Victorian times through to parties arriving by motor coach and car via the A9 Great North Road, which has nowadays been relegated to 'B'-road status as the modern A9 bypasses the village altogether. The pictures are arranged in a generally south-east to north-west direction, beginning with the spectacular Pass of Killiecrankie and ending at the foot of the Drumochter Pass through the Grampians.

Further Reading

The following were the principal books, newspapers and websites used by the author during his research. None are available from Stenlake Publishing; please contact your local bookshop, reference library or search for them on the internet.

Cecil J. Allen, *The Locomotive Exchanges 1870-1948*
Francis H Groome, *Ordnance Gazetteer of Scotland*, 1882
H. A. Vallance, *The Highland Railway*, 1969
Slater's Royal National Commercial Directory of Scotland 1886
Perthshire Advertiser
Perthshire Constitutional & Journal
The Scotsman
Atholl Estates: atholl-estates.co.uk
The Atholl Glens: athollglens.com
Blair Castle: blair-castle.co.uk
The Castles of Scotland: thecastlesofscotland.co.uk
Historic Environment Scotland: historicenvironment.scot
Lude Estate: ludeestate.co.uk

The vastness and grandeur of the area around the Pass of Killiecrankie can be judged in this 1905 picture of Fonnbhuic (pronounced 'Fonvuick') on the western side of the Pass. Ben Vrackie (2,759 feet) is in the background and the River Garry runs through the valley between it and the hill in the foreground. These buildings still stand today.

WISHING STONE, PASS OF KILLIECRANKIE.   A.7380

The Wishing Stone in the Pass of Killiecrankie is located in a precarious position on the very edge of a path above a 90-foot drop down to the River Garry. It's actually the top of the rock beneath protruding through the soil and was heart-shaped until the right curve of the heart was broken by parties of American tourists in the 1930s who chipped off pieces of the stone for souvenirs. The reason for it becoming known as the wishing stone is unclear but it is supposed by many people who have wished upon it to be an old Highland custom and to have the remarkable power of making their wishes come true. Past visitors are said to have included Queen Victoria, the King of Uganda and several MPs. During the Second World War a party of 200 Poles visited the Pass and each one in turn stood on the stone and cried out, 'Hitler'. Their wishes were unexpressed but were easily guessed, and eventually granted.

This single-track railway in the Pass of Killiecrankie near the Soldier's Leap was completed in 1863 for the Inverness & Perth Junction Railway by engineer Joseph Mitchell. Here, it is crossing the 109-yards-long, ten-span castellated stone Killiecrankie Viaduct which stands 54 feet above the River Garry, each arch being 35 feet wide. The viaduct doesn't actually cross the river; instead it runs alongside on very steep ground on the north-east bank (this is shown in the picture on the inside front cover). Immediately after the viaduct the line enters Killiecrankie Tunnel before emerging at the site of the former Killiecrankie station.

A southbound passenger train, double-headed by two Highland Railway locomotives, entering Killiecrankie station. When the station opened in 1865 it had minimal facilities, just a platform for the single line, but in 1896 a loop was built and new platforms and station buildings were provided, together with two signal boxes. This station was closed to passenger traffic on 3 May 1965 but the overbridge in the photograph, which carries a minor road over to the west bank of the River Garry, remains to mark its site.

A southbound train to Perth is waiting in Killiecrankie station in August 1915, its locomotive blowing off steam impatiently as it waits for a northbound train for Inverness to come off the single line and into the other platform. It shouldn't have too long to wait as the lower-quadrant semaphore signal has been cleared for the northbound train's arrival. The locomotive appears to be a 'Duke' Class 4-4-0; these were designed by David Jones and built between 1874 and 1878. The leading vehicle is a four-wheeled guard's van followed by a train of six-wheeled passenger carriages.

As can be seen in this 1933 photograph, the post office in Killiecrankie doubled as a tearoom, though both were closed some years ago. The van is selling fruit and vegetables and the car registration TJ416 is for Liverpool; the vehicle probably belonged to a family on holiday. The post office building is nowadays the privately-owned Old Post Office Cottage but the scene today on the former Great North Road looks almost the same.

Not exactly most people's idea of a cottage, Killiecrankie Cottage is an extensive rubble-built house designed by prominent architect William Burn for James Hay and built from 1825 onwards. It is a villa of 'cottage ornee' style, single-storey and attic, with dormers of an interesting design and a diagonally placed porch. It stands on the hillside overlooking the Soldier's Leap, one of a number of villas adorning the sides of the valley above the pass. The Tenandry estate on which it stands had historically been in the possession of the Stewarts of Tenandry, a branch of the Stewarts of Shearglass. When a later Mrs Hay died in 1980 aged 82, the estate passed to her daughters, Miss Christian Hay Stewart and Miss Charlotte Alston Stewart, who were liferent proprietors. The estate was acquired in 1902 by Sir William Stewart Dick-Conyngham, Bart., on the death of his great-aunt, Miss Charlotte Alston Stewart, and he sold it in 1911 to Captain William Thomas Shaw, a London stockbroker. The house was usually rented out to tenants; among them were the popular and sometimes controversial author Miss Marie Corelli (real name Mary Mackay) and her half-brother Eric Mackay who rented the villa for the summer of 1896, and the famous author of *Peter Pan*, J. M. Barrie, who rented it as a summer residence for a few weeks in 1922.

Druimuan House at Killiecrankie was designed by Andrew Heighton (Junior), and built in 1863 for Major Raymond Inglis. It was extended on the west side in 1877, again by Heighton (Junior), and subsequently a further extension to the east was completed in 1907. The photograph shows a two-storey, five-bay Scots-Baronial mansion with bellcast-roofed entrance tower and corbelled turret. It is set in 2½ acres of grounds and in the late twentieth century it was operated for some years as a bed-and-breakfast establishment before being purchased in 1995 for £400,000, becoming a private residence. The hill in the background, which rises to 2,369 feet, is Meall an' Daimh.

The Great North Road at Killiecrankie

The Great North Road in Scotland was formerly the A9 main road which passed through most towns and villages on its way northwards from Edinburgh to John O'Groats. South of Perth its importance has been diminished since the 1960s and 1970s by the construction of the M9 and M90 motorways and the Forth Road Bridge, while further north the road has become a mixture of single and dual carriageways as it bypassed nearly every town and village, leaving them served by B-grade roads. Much of the road followed the line of an ancient droving route. This became General Wade's military road in the eighteenth century, allowing military access to the Highlands, with further development from 1740 by Major William Caulfield. It was improved again in the nineteenth century by Thomas Telford although a tarmac surface was not laid over the whole route until 1929.

The Garry Guest House and Restaurant at Killiecrankie is seen here in August 1939, standing above the A9 main road, which is nowadays the B8079, in a position that affords lovely views across the River Garry. The motor car looks to be a four-door Austin 10/4 Cambridge model and its registration plate shows that it was registered in the Plymouth area. After the Second World War the establishment simply became the Garry Guest House and was later turned into a five-bedroomed private house, which it remains today. The restaurant has been tastefully reconstructed into a separate residential bungalow with attic bedrooms.

A cow gazes meditatively at the Great North Road running through the tiny hamlet of Aldclune, a mile beyond Killiecrankie, as local women go about their business. One of the oldest settlements in the area, Aldclune lies on the north bank of the River Garry and is bisected vertically by the Allt Cluain burn. At the eastern edge of the hamlet is the site of the Battle of Killiecrankie. There was an old chapel at one time at Aldclune but its site is now a garden in which two crosses are pointed out as marking the graves of English officers who died of wounds received in the battle. Most of the houses were built in the middle of the nineteenth century for retired Atholl estate workers and usually had two fields to form a smallholding to supplement their pensions. These joined the twenty houses already built in the 1700s and the hamlet used to have a blacksmith, joiner, corn mill, weavers and even its own school. The house on the right of the picture is Atholl Cottage and the building across the way was the blacksmith's shop, nowadays a ruin with only its walls standing to a low height. Both stand on the east side of the burn.

The Great North Road used to run through Aldclune but in 1927 the hamlet was bypassed when a new section was built on the Edinburgh to Inverness road which was by then designated the A9. This in turn was superseded in the 1980s when a new A9 was built that bypassed the whole area and the old A9 was downgraded to become the B8079. Aldclune's population had a reputation for longevity and in 1934 the *Perthshire Advertiser* reported that 'the population numbers only about 30. Four are over 80, their aggregate ages totalling 334 years; four are over 70, four over 65 and four over 60. During the last 40 years there has only been one death of a person under 50.' Even today the majority of the residents are elderly retirees. In this photograph the two Edwardian ladies and a gentleman are enjoying the sunshine outside Rose Cottage which stands on the west side of the Allt Cluain. They may be discussing the latest improvement to the village because in March 1909 the *Perthshire Advertiser* reported that 'The village of Aldclune, which was formerly dependent for its supply upon the burn passing through the village, has now been provided with an excellent supply. Throughout the village, at convenient points, 'stand-up' pipes have been provided and in some instances the householders have provided themselves with special connections and taps near or inside the house.' Luxury indeed!

Glen Fender is about five miles roughly north-north-west of Killiecrankie and runs in a generally west-south-west direction. The Fender Burn, which features several waterfalls, runs down its length until it joins the River Tilt. Middlebridge, pictured here, is a hamlet on the south bank of the burn near its confluence with the river but, despite its name, it doesn't have a bridge!

Tirinie House, about two miles from Blair Atholl, occupies a prominent situation at the end of a long single track road high up on the hill slopes in Glen Fender; Meall Gruaim (378 feet) is behind the house. It was built by architect Oswald Milne in 1923 and had fine marble chimneypieces and very high quality furnishings, particularly the barley-sugar balusters to stairs and lattice screens below. It was the home of Lady Helen Stewart Murray, a daughter of the 7th Duke of Atholl, who married David Alexander Tod in 1916 and moved into it on its completion. Tod died in 1933 and his wife the following year. The house was bequeathed and endowed by them 'for the establishment of a Home of Rest … with preference to persons directly engaged in the clerical, medical, surgical, or artistic professions, or their relatives.' The building had accommodation for ten persons and opened in 1938 as 'a home for rest and change of air for the professional classes', going on to provide a blissful retreat for stressed-out ministers, doctors and lawyers for nearly 60 years. The house is seen here in 1950, shortly before Miss Margery Moorwood set up an art studio in part of the building. Unfortunately, by the 1990s the home had begun to run at a loss and in 1998 the Court of Session agreed that the house and grounds should be put on the market after hearing that valuable paintings and furniture had already been sold to keep the wolf from the door. The house has since become privately owned.

The original Lude House was situated high up in Glen Fender but in the seventeenth century a new house named 'Pitnacree' was built on the present site about a mile east-north-east of Bridge of Tilt. From the beginning of the fourteenth century the lands of Lude belonged to the Robertsons of Lude, a branch of the Clan Donnachaidh. They had long-running feuds with the Earls and Dukes of Atholl and also became involved in the 1715 and 1745 Jacobite rebellions, entertaining Bonnie Prince Charlie at the house during his march south in 1745. The family was subsequently so heavily fined by the government for this that they had to sell the estate. In 1820 it was purchased by the McInroy family, who had made a fortune in British Guiana from sugar plantations, and they developed the estate and the village of Bridge of Tilt. 'Pitnacree' was demolished and the present Lude House was completed in Jacobethan style by the architect William Burn in 1839 for James Patrick McInroy. The estate later went to his grandson William, whose two sons predeceased him; with no male heirs to inherit the estate, it was acquired by Mr W. Gordon Gordon of London. After serving in the Second World War his son, William Gordon Gordon, purchased further land at Loch Vaeligan and set about developing the estate for farming, forestry and sport. His eldest son and grandson now run the estate.

A bridge over the River Tilt had been built in the sixteenth century about one and a half miles upstream of the present bridge. It was upgraded in the 1720s by General Wade whose military road had struck out north-westwards a mile beyond Aldclune to bridge the River Tilt at this point. This hamlet, named Old Bridge of Tilt, grew up by the bridge and today is a mixture of stylish old and new houses and villas built in traditional style. The long building in the middle of the picture was the mill and the white buildings seen in the distance above it are in Middlebridge.

Perth Road, Blair Atholl

In 1822 a new bridge was built downstream across the River Tilt when the Great North Road was diverted from General Wade's military road, and the present-day village of Bridge of Tilt grew up alongside it on the north bank of the River Garry. The approach to the village from the east, along the main road which became the A9 and is nowadays the B8079, is seen here in 1909, flanked by these substantial stone villas which culminated in the impressive St Andrew's church.

The row of villas in the previous picture ended with Robertson's confectionery and fancy goods shop and next to it was Rudlan's shop, nowadays a private house: they are seen here in the 1930s. Beyond them is St Andrew's Free Church which was built in 1855 and replaced an earlier wooden church which had been built at Kings Island, south of Blair Atholl, at the time of the 'Disruption' in 1843 but had become liable to flooding. In 1900 St Andrew's became part of the United Free Church and remained so until 1929 when the U.F. Church merged with the Established Church to become the Church of Scotland. There was already a church across the river in Blair Atholl and eventually the decision was taken to adopt that church as the area's main church and to demolish St Andrew's. The main building was removed in 1968, followed in 1971 by the tower. Only the vestry building now remains and the site is now a restful garden.

THE TERRACE, BRIDGE OF TILT 1011

These substantial and attractive villas with extensive gardens and lovely pastoral views are located on the southern outskirts of Bridge of Tilt and are collectively called The Terrace. This picture is dated 1917 but the foreground area and the pastoral views are almost unchanged today.

The Bridge of Tilt Hotel, a former hunting lodge built in 1840, is in the foreground of this picture. It has since been extended on both sides but there is still a large space in front of the hotel, very convenient for car parking. Unfortunately the hotel has been closed for many years, becoming an eyesore, but the local council approved plans in 2019 to refurbish it, including partial demolition, and to build five cottages in its grounds. This work was still ongoing at the time of writing. Beyond the hotel is Invertilt Road, then a terrace of very smart private houses with walled gardens which end with the present-day Tilt Stores. St Andrew's church, standing on the main road into Bridge of Tilt, completes the picture.

The Pavilion, Golf Course, Blair Atholl

Blair Atholl golf course is actually across the river in Bridge of Tilt and is located at the end of Invertilt Road. The club was founded in 1896 and its nine-hole course was designed by the celebrated James Braid. This picture shows Edwardian female golfers playing in front of the 'Pavilion', which is actually the clubhouse. Nowadays its veranda has been enclosed to provide a covered seating area overlooking the course and a terrace has been built in front of it. The course was converted to eighteen holes after the First World War but reverted to nine during the Second. It is nowadays a nine-hole, par 35 course and going round twice gives a par 70 course of 5,780 yards in length.

This new bridge over the River Tilt, with three segmental arches and triangular cutwaters, was designed by engineer John Mitchell and opened on 16 September 1822. The Great North Road was re-routed over this bridge, thereby bypassing the old bridge over the Tilt and the small village of Blair, nowadays called Old Blair. The Blair Atholl public school on the far side of the bridge, seen here in 1909, was built in 1833, extended in 1849 and extended again in 1875 when a new classroom was added. In 1873 there were 135 pupils of school age in the parish; in 1879 there was accommodation at the school for 187 pupils and an average attendance of 105. The school, nowadays a primary school, is now located in a newer building in St Adamnam Road in Bridge of Tilt, and has a capacity of 50 pupils although a census in 2015 revealed an average of only 24 pupils on the school register. The old school building now houses the Atholl Country Life Museum.

Passing further along the road, an avenue on the right leads up to Blair Castle which is said to have been started in 1269 by John Comyn, Lord of Badenoch. He was a neighbour of David Strathbogie, Earl of Atholl, and started building a tower on the earl's land while he was away on a crusade. On his return the earl complained to King Alexander I, won back his land and incorporated the tower into his own castle. The earldom passed through a number of hands until John Murray, son of the 2nd Earl of Tullibardine, was created Earl of Atholl in 1629; the title has remained in the Murray family ever since. In the 1640s the Murrays supported the Royalist cause and Cromwell's army took the castle following its invasion of Scotland in 1650. The restored King Charles II created the title Marquess of Atholl for John Murray, 2nd Earl of Atholl, and the title Duke of Atholl was granted to the 2nd Marquess in 1703. When Viscount Dundee launched the first Jacobite rising in 1689, the castle was held for the Catholic King James II and on 26 July Dundee and the clan chiefs held a council of war there. The following day they were victorious over the English army at Killiecrankie, but because Dundee was killed the Highland army melted away and King William of Orange's throne was safe. During the 1745 rebellion the castle was occupied twice by Bonnie Prince Charlie's army, firstly during its advance into England in September 1745 and then on its retreat north in February 1746. In 1740 the 2nd Duke had begun transforming the castle into a grand Georgian house. The apartments to the south were added in the mid-eighteenth century and the south-east range, incorporating the clock tower, was rebuilt after a fire in 1814. In 1872 the 7th Duke remodelled the exterior back to its original appearance and a new entrance hall was erected. A ballroom wing was added in 1885. During the Great War the castle was used as an auxiliary hospital and after 1922 the family found it more convenient to live in the private apartments. The castle has been open to the public since 1936.

The Atholl Highlander regiment was first raised in Perthshire as the 77th Regiment of Foot by John Murray, 4th Duke of Argyll, in 1777. It was disbanded in 1783 but in 1839 George Murray, Lord Glenlyon and subsequently the 6th Duke of Atholl, re-formed the regiment as his personal bodyguard. Nowadays it is the only remaining private army in Europe. In 1842 the regiment escorted Queen Victoria during her tour of Perthshire and two years later, when the Queen stayed at the castle, the regiment mounted the guard for the duration of her stay. In recognition of this service the Queen announced in 1845 that she would present the Atholl Highlanders with colours, thus giving the regiment official status in perpetuity. The regiment is made up of specially selected employees of the Duke and is not part of the British Army, being used only for ceremonial purposes. The present Colonel-in-Chief is Bruce George Ronald Murray, 12th Duke of Atholl, and every May bank holiday weekend the regiment parades in front of the castle wearing the kilts and plaids of the Murray of Atholl tartan and is reviewed by the Duke. The regiment also parades at several other events including some abroad.

The Atholl Gathering features the parade on the Saturday of the May bank holiday, followed by Highland games on the Sunday. This photograph of the event from Edwardian times shows the busy refreshment stall, the customers displaying an interesting range of headgear and other types of clothing of the era.

Old Blair is a tiny village of eighteenth century stone cottages adjoining and overlooking the grounds of Blair Castle. The building on the left in this photograph is Old Blair Lodge, formerly an inn, which is set in the village a few hundred yards from Blair Castle and is now a seven-bedroom self-catering holiday house. The former village manse on the right has been transformed into a boutique hotel called the Old Manse of Blair. The village lies near the junction of three ancient routes to the north. The narrow road at the gate to the churchyard is named Minigaig Street and is the start of the centuries-old path, the Minigaig, which ran from Atholl along Glen Bruar to Badenoch and which fell into comparative disuse after General Wade routed his road over Drumochter for soldiers to pass on their way to the Hanoverian Ruthven Barracks outside Kingussie. It was not completely abandoned, however, as drovers used it as recently as the early years of the nineteenth century, no doubt a legacy of the period when the tolls at Dalnacardoch on the Wade road made the Minigaig preferable.

An Edwardian scene in Old Blair village. The cottages are still there today.

The ruins of the fifteenth century St Bride's Kirk at Old Blair stand on a mound within the grounds of Blair Castle. Seen here from the south-east, it was the original church of Blair Atholl parish until it was replaced in 1824 by a new building in Blair Atholl village, but the burial ground is still used and is the historic burial place of the Dukes of Atholl. The structure probably dates back to a major reconstruction of an existing church following the Reformation in 1560 but the church's origins go back much further. St Bride's Kirk first enters the written record in 1275 when it contributed 32 shillings in tithes or taxes to help fund the Crusades. After receiving mortal wounds at the Battle of Killiecrankie, Viscount Dundee was buried three days later in the vault of the church. A plaque on the inside of the south wall of the building records his interment below. Around 1794 the grave was opened for another interment and legend has it that the gravedigger removed his armour and sold it to a party of tinkers. Whether or not this is true, his breastplate and part of his helmet were recovered and are now displayed at Blair Castle. He was immortalised in Sir Walter Scott's novel *Old Mortality* (1816) and in a popular poem Scott wrote in 1829 to the old Scottish air of *Bonnie Dundee*. Ever since then the viscount has been known as 'Bonnie Dundee'. The rubble-built kirk is now roofless but its walls are almost complete although they have been considerably altered over the years and have nowadays been cleared of ivy. This photograph dates from around the 1880s.

This curious hermitage, about which little is known, stands on the west bank of the River Tilt opposite a little cascade and not far from Blair Castle. Below it there is a deep pool into which, in days gone by, adulterers were thrown, sewed up in a sack, and drowned.

Returning to the main road through Blair Atholl and just beyond the avenue up to Blair Castle, this 1909 picture shows the Scottish Horse Hall and Tullibardine Institute which was built in 1906/07 as a drill hall for the Scottish Horse. The crest of the Scottish Horse Regiment is on the armorial plaque above the entrance. The regiment was originally established in 1900 when the Marquis of Tullibardine, heir to the 7th Duke of Atholl, was asked by Lord Kitchener to raise a regiment of Scotsmen and men of Scottish descent in South Africa during the Second Boer War. The men soon saw active service against the Boers in the Western Transvaal and a second regiment of Scottish Horse was also raised by the duke. A third regiment was created in August 1914 on the outbreak of the First World War and the following month all three regiments became the Scottish Horse Mounted Brigade. They subsequently went through several reorganisations and changes of name until 1956 when they were amalgamated with the Fife and Forfar Yeomanry. The building served as a drill hall in both world wars. Today, as the Village Hall, the building has many uses including being the practise venue for the Blair Atholl Pipe Band.

The Scottish Horse, as a local yeomanry, would assemble each summer for training at Blair Atholl. Here, some of the regiment are seen relaxing at their summer camp in the early years of the twentieth century.

This impressive range of buildings stands in Atholl Square, filling the space between the Tullibardine Institute and the Atholl Arms Hotel. The sign on the front of the shop in the centre of the picture is that of J. Seaton, bootmaker and saddler. This business closed in 1975 when Alistair Seaton retired and the shop has since been a gun shop, a computer business, an architect's office and, in 2021, is the premises of Barry Sanderson Heating and Plumbing. Happily, the muddy area in front of the buildings is now a well-kept public lawn. The post office, with a bay window, is on the extreme right of the photograph, just round the corner in Ford Road. This is now the Blair Atholl Surgery and the post office is located within the Premier Atholl Convenience Store a little further down Ford Road.

The Blair Atholl shop of the family business of McKerchar and Macnaughton Limited, milliners and drapers, whose headquarters were in Aberfeldy and whose business ran through three generations. A partnership was formed in the 1880s between James Macnaughton and Peter McKerchar and grew to become a business comprising licensed supermarket, department store including tailoring, and various other enterprises, with branches in Kinloch Rannoch, Pitlochry and Blair Atholl. Four travelling shops serviced the surrounding glens. The business was sold in 1984 and nowadays its premises in Atholl Square are occupied by Highlands Jewellery, though the facade looks the same apart from the change of name.

The foundation stone for the Atholl Arms Hotel in the centre of Blair Atholl village, seen here in 1907, was laid by the 4th Duke of Atholl on 23 June 1830 and the hotel was completed in 1832. Tall bay-windowed wings were added in 1854, followed by a ballroom in 1856, used by the Duke of Atholl for his private entertainments and for the Atholl Gatherings. A further building at the rear, added in 1877, formed the buildings into a rectangle and completed the courtyard. The hotel was a staging post on the road from London to Inverness and was visited in 1844 by Queen Victoria. Both old and new forms of transport are seen in this 1907 photograph: a top-hatted driver sits patiently awaiting his master while what looks to be a Daimler saloon motor car with solid tyres stands near the front door. The bowling green in the foreground is long gone; nowadays its site is an empty space in front of the road to the railway station. In 1985 a £250,000 refurbishment was interrupted when its owner fled to Spain, having incurred unpaid debts of £230,000. Luckily, the building then came under new ownership with support from the Duke of Atholl; the work was completed and the hotel was reopened by the Duke the following year. It has been upgraded a number of times since then.

The Blair Atholl war memorial, located across the road from the Atholl Arms Hotel, was built by Robert Robertson of Aldclune and unveiled on 18 May 1924 by the Duke of Atholl. A large assembly attended the solemn ceremony which took place in glorious sunshine. The memorial takes the form of a massive 20-ton monolith of natural rock which was hewn from Craigy Barns Hill on the Atholl Estates near Dunkeld and its base is surrounded by heather. The inscription on the stone says only '1914 – 1918' but three plaques are set into the wall on three sides of its enclosure. Two of them list the names of the 47 men who fell in the First World War while the third lists the names of the fourteen servicemen and one civilian who died in the Second.

Garryside Cottages are two rows of dwellings at the end of Ford Road, which runs between the side of the Atholl Arms Hotel and the Square, down to the River Garry. The area is a large, planned cottage community of one and two-storey rubble-built houses with picturesque overhanging eaves and gables. The houses were designed in 1856 by architects R. & R. Dickson, initially to house servants from Blair Atholl castle though by the 1890s this had been widened to include many more tradesmen from the village. The footbridge across the River Garry replaced both the old ford at the end of Ford Road and its successor, a three-arch stone bridge that was built in 1737 but washed away six months later by a severe flood. In June 1991 this footbridge was replaced with a new 40-metre structure which utilised the old masonry piers; the one in mid-river is inscribed with the footbridge's construction date of 1865 and a plaque on the opposite pier records that the bridge was rebuilt by the 225 (Birmingham) Field Squadron of the Royal Monmouthshire Royal Engineers (Militia) under the Military Aid to the Civilian Community scheme.

Many of the buildings and scenes described on previous pages can be seen in this panoramic view of Blair Atholl. The River Garry runs through the foreground from left to right and is joined on the left by the Banvie Burn which runs down from the side of the ghostly-white Blair Castle. The main road through the village crosses the burn just before its confluence with the Garry and very soon comes to the railway station where a train made up of Highland Railway carriages is standing at the southbound platform. The station approach road sweeps in a curve down to the main road past the side of the Atholl Arms Hotel and the site of its erstwhile bowling green. The hotel frontage faces the main road and on its far side Ford Road runs past the Blair Atholl watermill (adjacent to the fork in the road) and down to the Garry, with the planned settlement of Garryside Cottages at its foot. Returning to the main road, the next set of buildings with towers are the backs of the shops in Atholl Square but the adjacent Tullibardine Institute is hidden by trees. Looking further to the right, the River Tilt is flowing down Glen Tilt to its confluence (just out of the picture) with the River Garry. The 'new' road bridge of 1822 is in the middle distance while the 150-foot lattice girder railway bridge designed by Joseph Mitchell, with castellated stone abutments placed at either end to please the Duke of Atholl, was built in 1863.

From 9 to 19 July 1937 Girl Guides from all parts of the British Isles, and every country in Europe except Germany, Russia and Italy, gathered at Blair Atholl for the first international guides' camp held in Scotland. Three hundred girls, made up of 200 from Britain and 100 from overseas countries, were joined on Visitors Day by a contingent of 1,500 Perthshire guides. The Committee of the World Association of Girl Guides and Girl Scouts led by Lady Baden-Powell, together with Chief Commissioners from all corners of the globe, attended and were accommodated in Blair Castle. On Visitors Day, in lovely weather, the visitors were entertained by a programme in which representatives of twenty countries took part. Dances and songs were rendered in national costumes, and in a silent drill demonstration orders were given by sign only, which were understood by all participants, thus obviating difficulty on the part of those who couldn't speak English.

The Society of Miniature Rifle Clubs was formed early in 1903 from the merger of the Society of Working Men's Rifle Clubs and the British Rifle League and its first meeting in Scotland took place in Perth in 1909. The Mid-Atholl Miniature Rifle Club were the Perthshire League Champions in 1912 and in this photograph were about to celebrate their success with a bottle of Grandtully whisky. Hopefully they unloaded their rifles first!

Blair Atholl railway station, 35 miles north of Perth, opened on 9 September 1863 on the Inverness & Perth Junction Railway. From that date until 1893 it was named 'Blair Athole' before gaining its present name. One of the first users of the station was Queen Victoria who arrived in a special royal train only six days after the line's opening, on a visit to Blair Castle to see her long-standing friend George Murray, 6th Duke of Atholl, who was dying of cancer. The present 'B' listed station dates from 1869 and its design had to be approved by the 7th Duke of Atholl because it serves Blair Castle. The canopy still survives today but the near gable was demolished in the 1970s. The station originally had a 770-yards-long passing loop which was flanked by the two platforms but this has since been extended northbound as double track as far as Dalwhinnie.

Blair Atholl railway station, 1918, with a southbound train headed by 4-6-0 No. 140 *Taymouth Castle* approaching. Note there are two goods wagons between the locomotive and the passenger carriages – this was common practice on the Highland Railway at that time. This station lies at the foot of the long northbound climb with a continuous steep gradient up to Druimuachdar (Drumochter) summit just beyond the former Dalnaspidal station, 1,484 feet above sea level and the highest main line summit in Britain. Northbound trains were given an assisting engine at Blair Atholl to help them up 'The Hill': either a pilot engine was attached to the front of the train or a banker was attached to the rear. There was an intermediate station at Struan. An amusing incident occurred in 1948 when the newly formed British Railways was testing locomotives from its constituent companies to see which was best suited to various routes. The former Southern Railway supplied one of its 'West Country' Class 4-6-2 Pacifics, No. 34004 *Yeovil*, which was tested on the 4 p.m. train from Perth to Inverness with a 380-ton train. At Blair Atholl an ex-Caledonian Railway 4-4-0 was attached as banker to assist this locomotive from the supposedly 'sissy' south of England. Cecil J. Allen, the well-known railway author, wrote that 'with such terrific vigour did the train engine start away that not only was a speed of 46 m.p.h. reached [on the steep gradient], but the effect was to wind the banker, which required every bit of the standing time at Struan to recover breath!'

Cecil J. Allen continued: 'It was now the turn of the banker's crew to demonstrate that the honour of the Highland must be maintained. In brief, the two engines cut the 31-minute allowance from Struan up to Dalnaspidal to less than 19½ minutes!' The honour of the Highland Railway had indeed been restored! Struan railway station, seen here in 1915, was opened on 9 September 1863 and closed on 3 May 1965, a victim of the 'Beeching Cuts'. It was a two-platform station just west of the River Garry; its main station buildings were on the northbound platform with smaller ones on the southbound. The original main, rather plain buildings were replaced after a fire in 1898 by the ones in this photograph. The station buildings were demolished when the station was closed but the platforms remain. The station originally had two signal boxes but these were replaced by a single box when the line was doubled in 1900. Just to the south of the station is the Struan Inn from where a coach service ran from the station to Kinloch Rannoch, about twelve miles south-west.

The unusual siting of the railway bridges just south of Struan station was determined by the prohibition of crossing the River Garry at any other point within the parks of Blair Castle. The northbound stone railway bridge, with an 80 foot middle span crossing the road bridge and decorated with castellations and arrow slits, was built in 1863 and the southbound girder rail bridge in 1900 when the line was doubled from Blair Atholl to Dalnacardoch signal box. The road bridge they cross at an angle was probably built around 1765 and is the former turnpike road, nowadays the B847, which goes up Glen Errochty to Kinloch Rannoch. They are locally known collectively as the 'Three Bridges' and mark the boundary between the settlements of Struan and Calvine. Both Calvine (which means 'Smooth Wood' in Gaelic) and Struan ('Little Stream') are historic names. The former's name certainly pre-dates 1863 but Struan dates back to the fifteenth century with Robert Duncanson, 4th Chief of Clan Donnachaidh, having been created feudal baron of that airt in 1451.

The School, Calvine 1075

Named the Struan District School, this school at Calvine was opened by Lady Helen Stewart Murray of Blair Castle on 11 November 1909 and replaced one at nearby Pittagowan. Lady Helen encouraged everyone who knew Gaelic to try and keep it up, and to speak it in their homes and learn to read and write it. This photograph was taken soon after the school opened and shows fifteen boys and thirteen girls, plus their teacher, Miss M'Leod. Calvine is approximately five miles west of Blair Atholl, on the B847 close to the village of Old Struan The school was later called Struan Primary School and located in a modern building that was built in front of the old school. However, the school was closed in 2017 and its pupils transferred to Blair Atholl Primary School.

Standing on the B847 and seen here in 1924, these cottages in the centre of Calvine village have since been modernised but are still recognisable today. The hut at the far end has since become a public toilet.